I AM SPECIAL

PRIMARY

WRITTEN BY LINDA SCHWARTZ   ILLUSTRATED BY BEV ARMSTRONG

The Learning Works

P.O. Box 6187 Santa Barbara, CA 93160

THIS BOOK BELONGS

TO

_____

The purchase of this book entitles the individual teacher to
reproduce copies for use in the classroom.

Contents

Introduction

I AM SPECIAL offers an exciting and motivating way for primary children to keep a journal about themselves throughout the year. The book is divided into twelve sections, with two exercises in each section. Children can complete the sections at their own pace according to age and ability level. The pages may be kept in a folder as work progresses and then bound as a book at the end of the school or calendar year or upon completion.

I AM SPECIAL provides opportunities for children to develop a positive self-image and better understanding of themselves. The topics presented offer children a chance to think more creatively, grow intellectually, and to learn to commnicate their thoughts and feelings.

Name _____

My Story

1. My name is _____.

2. Sometimes my family calls me _____.
   (nickname)

3. I live at _____.
   (address)

4. I am _____ years old.

5. There are _____ in my family counting me.

6. I am the _____ oldest _____ youngest _____ in the middle.

7. I am _____ tall and weigh _____.

8. One thing that makes me very special is _____

   _____.

9. Check (✔) the best answers.

I am
_____ right-handed
_____ left-handed

My hair is
_____ long
_____ short
_____ medium

_____ curly
_____ straight
_____ thick
_____ thin

I do _____ do not _____ wear glasses.

Name_____

A Picture of Me

This is how I look at the beginning of the school year.

(Draw your picture here.)

Name _____

My Handwriting

Copy this in either printing or cursive writing.

This is a sample of my best handwriting. I will save it. At the end of the school year I will look at it again. Then I will see how my writing has improved.

Name _____

My Goals for the Year

This year in school I would like to do better in

1. _____

2. _____

3. _____

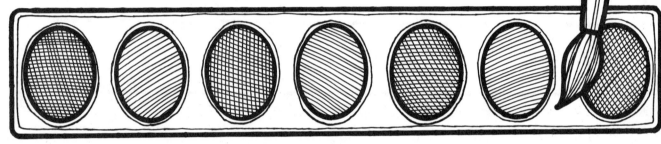

I would like to do better in art.

This year at home I would like to try harder to

1. _____

2. _____

3. _____

I would like to try harder to have a good garden.

Name _____

The Strong Me

1. In school my best subject is_____.

2. The game or sport I play best is _____.

3. My friends think I am great at _____

   _____.

4. I know someone who is proud of me! That someone is

   _____. _____ is proud
          (name)   (She or He)

   of me because I _____.

5. These are the people I help:_____

   _____.

6. I can show_____ how to
                  (name)

   _____.

I can show my little sister Amy how to make a sandwich.

Name _____

My Special Interests

1. I enjoy collecting _____.

2. I take _____ lessons.

3. I belong to this club or group: _____.

4. I think it would be fun to learn more about _____

    _____.

5. I have fun doing:

    _____ at home

    _____ at school

    _____ with my friends

    _____ with my family

    _____ all by myself

I have fun playing with Sammy, my kitten, at home.

Name _____

Someone Special

(Pick someone in your family to tell about: your mother, father, grandmother, grandfather, aunt, or uncle.)

1. His/Her name is_____.

2. He/She helps me do these things: _____

   _____

   _____.

3. He/She is special to me because _____

   _____.

4. I like to go _____ with him/her.

5. His/Her favorites:

   Food _____   Book _____

   Hobby _____   T.V. Show _____

My aunt is special to me because she lets me help her bake cookies every Saturday.

Name _____

Brothers and Sisters

1. **I have a sister named** _____ Age _____

 _____ Age _____

_____ Age _____

2. **I have a brother named** _____ Age _____

 _____ Age _____

_____ Age _____

3. **Two things I enjoy doing with my brothers and sisters are:**

_____

_____.

4. **Brothers and sisters are fun because** _____

_____.

5. **Brothers and sisters are not so fun because** _____

_____.

6. **I don't have any brothers or sisters. This is the name of**

my friend who is like a brother _____. **This is**

the name of my friend who is like a sister _____.

7. **The best part about being an only child is** _____

_____.

Name _____

My Feelings About School

1. I am in the _____ grade.

2. The name of my school is_____.

3. My teacher's name is_____.

4. The best day I had in school this year was_____

_____.

5. The worst day I had in school this year was_____

_____.

6. I would not have had this bad day if_____

_____.

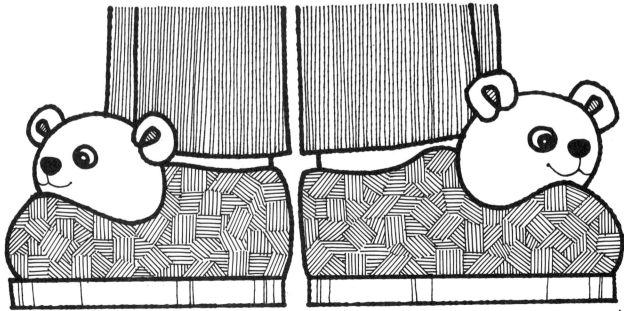

My worst day was the day I forgot to put my shoes on, and came to school in my slippers.

Name _____

If I Were the Teacher

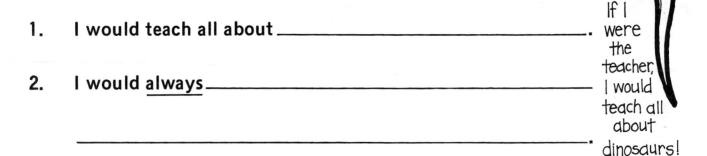

If I could be the teacher......

1. I would teach all about _____ .

2. I would <u>always</u> _____

    _____ .

3. I would <u>never</u> _____

    _____ .

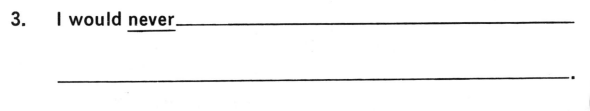

4. I would let all the kids_____ .

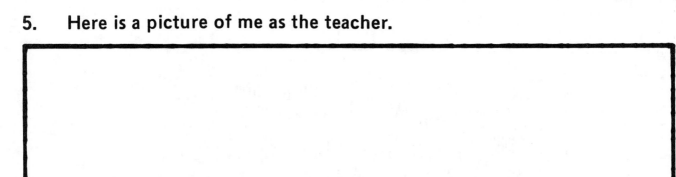

5. Here is a picture of me as the teacher.

```



```

14

Name _____

My Friend Flag

Picture 1 shows me with my best friends.

Picture 2 shows something my friends and I enjoy doing together.

Picture 3 shows one thing my friends and I like to talk about.

Picture 4 shows something my friends and I pretend we are.

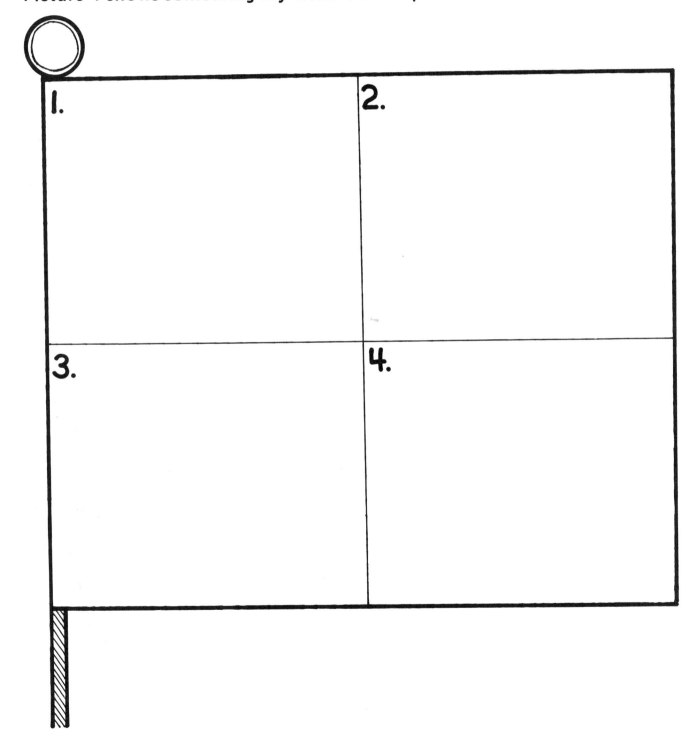

Name_____

Pick a Friend

If I could pick a friend.....

1.   **To sit next to at school it would be** _____.

2.   **To spend the night at my house it would be**_____.

3.   **To tell a secret to it would be**_____.

4.   **To get to know better it would be**_____.

5.   **To help me with my homework it would be**_____.

6.   **To be my brother it would be**_____.

7.   **To be my sister it would be**_____.

Name _____

My Favorite Foods

If I could eat whatever I wanted, I would have

_____ for breakfast

_____ for lunch

_____ for dinner

These are my favorites...

meat _____

vegetable _____

soup _____

candy _____

sandwich _____

fruit _____

cereal _____

ice cream _____

cookie _____

drink _____

I can cook these foods by myself:

_____

_____

_____

_____

Name _____

My Super Favorites

1. My favorite color is _____.

2. My favorite place is _____.

3. My favorite animal is _____.

4. My favorite sound is _____.

5. My favorite smell is _____.

My favorite animal is the giraffe.

6. Here are pictures of my favorite:

TV Show

Book

Name _____

Title _____

Movie

Title _____

Name _____

Special Feelings

1. On the first day of school, this is how I feel:

    _____

    _____.

2. When someone says something nice about me, this is how I feel:

    _____

    _____.

3. When I have a fight, this is how I feel:

    _____

    _____.

4. When I do something good, this is how I feel:

    _____

    _____.

When I have a fight I want to kick the ground and cry.

19

Name _____

 # My Many Feelings

I have many feelings.

1. One time I felt very sad when _____

    _____.

2. One time I felt very silly when _____

    _____.

3. One time I felt very scared when _____

    _____.

4. One time I felt very important when _____

    _____.

Here is a picture of the time I felt very important....

I AM SPECIAL
Copyright © 1978 — THE LEARNING WORKS   20

Name _____

The Real Me

I think I am ..... (✔ the best answers)

_____ quiet as a mouse

or

_____ noisy as a firecracker

_____ a little of both

_____ fast as a rabbit

or

_____ slow as a turtle

_____ a little of both

_____ super neat

or

_____ super messy

_____ a little of both

_____ an indoor kid

or

_____ an outdoor kid

_____ a little of both

_____ a talker

or

_____ a listener

_____ a little of both

The "ING" Me

1. **Here are three words that end in "ing" that tell about me:**

   a. _____

   b. _____

   c. _____

   singing

   asking

   sleeping

2. **Here are pictures of my three "ing" words:**

   jumping eating

   laughing

Name _____

The Famous Me of the Future

Someday I would like to read about myself in the newspaper.
I think it would be fun to be famous for

_____.

2.   Here is a newspaper story about the famous me.

☆DAILY NEWS ☆☆☆ SPECIAL EDITION☆

_____ IS FAMOUS!
(NAME)

Name _____

The Travel Bug

1.   I have been in these states:

_____.

2.   I have been to: (✔ those you have seen.)

a.   airport   _____   h.   museum   _____
b.   art gallery   _____   i.   zoo   _____
c.   ball game   _____   j.   planetarium   _____
d.   beach   _____   k.   train depot   _____
e.   mountains   _____   l.   bus station   _____
f.   park   _____   m.   library   _____
g.   circus   _____   n.   other   _____

3.   One place I would like to see in the future is_____

_____ because_____

_____.

4.   Here is a picture of the special place I would like to see.

_____

Name_____

A Picture of Me

This is how I look at the end of the school year.
(Draw your picture here.)

I don't look like I did at the beginning of the year. This is the
way I have changed:

____ I am taller.   ____ I have a tooth missing.

____ I am thinner.   ____ My hair is longer.

____ I am not as thin.   ____ My hair is shorter.

____ I have a tan.   ____ My hair is curled.

____ I have more freckles. ____ I have new glasses.

                           ____ I smile more.

Name _____

Imagine That!

Do you ever try dreaming when you are not asleep? Here are
some daydreams you can have fun with. Imagine that.....

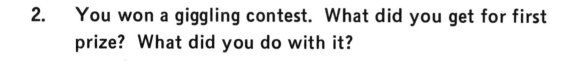

1.	You are flying your own airplane. Where would you go?
	Who would you take with you?

	_____

	_____.

2.	You won a giggling contest. What did you get for first
	prize? What did you do with it?

	_____

	_____.

3.	You cannot be <u>seen</u> by anyone, but you can see everyone
	else. What would you do all day?

	_____

	_____.

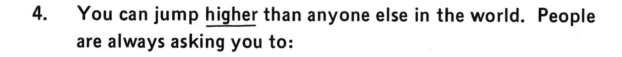

4.	You can jump <u>higher</u> than anyone else in the world. People
	are always asking you to:

	_____

	_____.

Name_____

What I Learned About Myself

1. Read page 4. Then check (✔) one:

   I did_____ did not _____ meet my goals.

2. I looked at my handwriting on page 3. I think my writing

   is _____ now.

3. I think I have improved this year in_____.

4. I was happy that I_____.

5. I still need to work on _____.

6. The one new thing I discovered about myself was_____

   _____.

7. This year I learned how to _____by myself.

8. If I could change one thing about myself it would be_____

   _____.

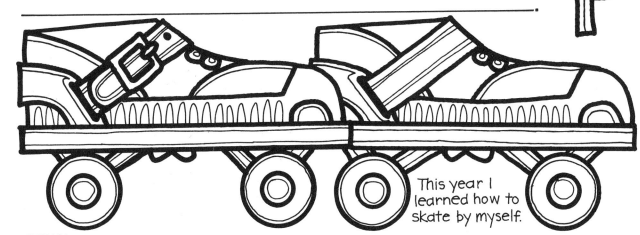

This year I learned how to skate by myself.

★★★ This ★★★
I AM SPECIAL
AWARD
is presented to

_____
(☺ a rather special person)

for completing all the pages of
"I AM SPECIAL".

_____ _____
Teacher's or Parent's Signature   Date

28